T0171591

The UNBROKEN *Home*

Patrick T Gorman

WESTBOW
PRESS
A DIVISION OF THOMAS NELSON

ISBN: 978-1-4497-6412-8 (sc)
ISBN: 978-1-4497-6413-5 (e book)
ISBN: 978-1-4497-7181-2 (hc)

Library of Congress Control Number: 2012915072

WestBow Press books may be ordered through booksellers or by contacting:

WestBow Press
A Division of Thomas Nelson
1663 Liberty Drive
Bloomington, IN 47403
www.westbowpress.com
1-(866) 928-1240

Because of the dynamic nature of the Internet, any web addresses or
links contained in this book may have changed since publication and
may no longer be valid. The views expressed in this work are solely those
of the author and do not necessarily reflect the views of the publisher,
and the publisher hereby disclaims any responsibility for them.

Any people depicted in stock imagery provided by Thinkstock are models,
and such images are being used for illustrative purposes only.

Certain stock imagery © Thinkstock.

Printed in the United States of America

WestBow Press rev. date: 10/12/2012

ABOUT THE AUTHOR

THE author of this book is a blue-collar mechanical contractor. He has a high school education with no formal training in theology or counseling. He is just an ordinary person that grew tired of day-to-day unhappiness. He grew up in an ordinary home and family. Today he is still just an ordinary person with a message of joy and hope from the Bible. God still uses ordinary people for His purposes. This author is one of those ordinary people.

Patrick T. Gorman Sr.

TABLE OF CONTENTS

PREFACE

*E*VERY day the social landscape is strewn with the debris of
one broken home after another. We have become compliant
with divorce, anger, resentment, and bitterness. It does not have
to be that way. I grew weary of the day-to-day pain and failure
in my own life and started looking for a better way. I almost gave
up on several occasions but am glad I didn't. This book is the
culmination of years of praying, reading, listening, struggling,
and finally finding some answers. I still have to go back and read
this book occasionally just to remind myself of the answers that
were so hard to find and can be easily forgotten in the heat of
the battle each day.

If you are married, both you and your spouse need to read this book. Save your discussions until you both have had time to digest the "recipe" in its pages. Let it speak to you individually and then collectively. Use the blank pages at the end of each chapter to make notes or record your own thoughts to help heal your home.

As long as there is breath in us, there is no situation that cannot be changed. The proof of this can be found in the pages of this book.

Like anything else in life, you have to want something badly enough to do whatever it takes to attain it. An unbroken home is worth all that it takes, and more. This is not a shortcut or a magic bullet that is going to fix everything. It is a format of a process that will get you to where you want to be. It will take work and patience, but the joy achieved will be astounding.

My prayer for you,

> *Lord, please let these words be a blessing to the home of the one reading them. I know you are in the healing business and if this home needs healing you can and will do it if we listen to your instructions and do it your way. So, Lord, bless the home of these readers and open their hearts and eyes to your truth. Thank you Lord for caring enough about us to send your Holy Spirit to guide and direct us to the place you have planned for us on this earth and beyond. Amen*

Take your time and enjoy the trip to a wonderful new life for you and your family!

".....as for me and my house, we will serve the Lord." - Joshua 24:15

ALL HOMES ARE BROKEN

WHAT is an unbroken home? An unbroken home is a place of joy and tranquillity. There is no strife, jealousy, malice, contention, or selfishness. It is a peaceful, secure sanctuary for all those that dwell there. It has a spirit of unity and unconditional love. It is the most sought after place in the entire world. It is as close as we can get to heaven on earth. It is a Garden of Eden and it is what God intended for us when he created us.

Do you know people that are always content and happy? What is their secret? How did they get that way? If you could see into their home, you would find a place of order and a power that is difficult to understand. We all want our homes to be this way, but how do we get there? It can be done. After years of pain and failure, I had given up on finding the answers. I was 58 years old when my wife and I finally learned the secret to this happiness. I hope you don't wait that long. Sadly, some will never find them. They will scoff at these words and go on down the hard road they have chosen. Some will even fight to hold onto their misery like I did. However, it does not have to be that way. You can choose to change the direction of your home any time you wish.

Imagine this. If I came to your door today and said I would give you any new vehicle of your choosing, free of charge, you would take it. But I'll do even more than that. If you are not pleased with the one you choose, you can come back and get another any time you wish. The only catch is that you have to let me destroy the old one. While this offer is "too good to be true", it is what we can do in our homes every day.

There is a recipe to use any time we want to "renovate" our homes and make them new. It does not cost anything except to give up our old ways and begin anew. Not only is it free but there is unlimited access to all the help you will need 24/7! So why don't people use this recipe? Because they don't know about it.

My first marriage of thirty-seven years failed, and my second was well on its way down the same path. My second marriage was my wife's fourth. Between us, we had experienced many years of misery and failure. We were determined to find some answers that would save us from another failure. We went to counseling, read books, went to our pastors, and listened to anyone that would try to help us to little or no avail. We became frustrated and were tempted to give up many times. I will share some of our trials later, but I want you to know that our home was as broken as it could be. But we kept searching and did not give up.

What we did not realize was, that while we were searching, God was feeding us one ingredient of the recipe at the time. As we applied each new ingredient of the recipe, we were being healed without even realizing it. One day we just stopped and looked back at God's creation and realized the miracle that had happened in our home.

Your home can be a place of magnificent wonder if you use God's recipe. He wrote it down and placed it at your fingertips and all you have to do is accept and apply it. Today, our home amazes us. It was a place of hate, selfishness, disrespect, distrust, anger, drug and sexual addiction, and total misery. Now it is a place of peace, love, devotion, integrity, and security, all because of a simple recipe. But don't be fooled. It was simple, but not easy! I will not mislead you to believe that this was or will be a cakewalk. There <u>will</u> be some pain.

A wise man once said that no one will change until the pain of change is less than the pain of where we are. If we had to endure twice the pain that we had to endure to get to where we are today, it would still be the best deal of our entire life.

There are no guarantees that you will succeed. In fact, the odds are against you. If you try to take a shortcut, or substitute fake ingredients, you will fail. If you sacrifice the truth for comfort, you will fail. We tried several times to take a shortcut and all it did was cripple our healing. If you give up and quit working at it, you will fail. This recipe is complete and exact and is the only recipe on the planet that is guaranteed to work.

Back to the new vehicle. Suppose your new vehicle arrives and you find out that some of the parts are counterfeit or defective. How fast would you bring it back? Suppose you find defects in every one you take home. You should not be surprised. This is an inherent problem, and cannot be avoided. A vehicle is made by humans and can never be perfect. Humans inhabit our homes, and the same applies there. Do you think God would bring you an imperfect vehicle that he designed and built? Of course not and He does not want you living a life with brokeness and pain. From this point forward, if you want this kind of life, you are going to have to choose between God's recipe and your own. Only one of you can be right. Sometimes you will easily agree with him. Other times (as I did) you will try to prove him wrong. One of the reasons I am writing this book is to help prevent you from falling into the same painful traps that I and others fell into along the way, and to help you find the answers God gives us for our healing. These traps can slow or completely block your healing if you let them.

All Homes Are Broken

The first step is to accept that all our homes have brokeness. It is not a matter of "if" our homes are broken, it is a matter of how much that our homes broken. The fact of the matter is that <u>all</u> homes are broken. If we examine our homes through unbiased eyes, we will be amazed at what we see. The good news is that they can be healed. Notice that I did not say fixed or repaired. You repair a washing machine or a car. You fix a broken window. The essence of people is that they are living beings. You cannot "fix" a person, but Jesus can and will heal the person. Jesus said in John 10: 10; "The thief cometh not but for to steal and kill, and to destroy; I am come that they might have life, and that they might have it more abundantly." (KJV) Out of his own mouth, He has identified the enemy and his intentions toward our homes and us. And he also says that He will help us to defeat the enemy! Jesus does not promise something that he does not do. Jesus was speaking of our lives and homes here and now.

If we accept that all homes are broken, then obviously, we are the products of broken homes ourselves. We sometimes refer to broken homes as only those that have a / missing parent or are incomplete in some way. The fact is that many homes that have both parents present are still damaged or broken. As we move forward, you will identify areas in your home that need healing. Some will be minor and easily addressed. Others may be complex and need more understanding and work. Don't let the size of the brokeness in your home bother you. This recipe is larger than any brokeness.

Regardless of how much we heal, Satan, as we speak, is hatching a plan to ambush your home again and again. In other words, this is spiritual warfare. The enemy never gives up and the home is his preferred battleground. He will come again and again. You may heal in one area but the enemy will surely attack and wound you in another. As this recipe unfolds, you will find brokeness you did not even know about, learn how to get it healed and how to protect your home from Satan's attacks.

In order to understand and how to use the recipe for healing, we need to understand the things that cause brokeness. Those things will be addressed in detail as we go along but we must look at how we got to where we are today.

Let's go back to the beginning. In Genesis God created Adam and Eve. He created Adam from the dust of the earth and "breathed life into him." He gave Adam dominion of all the earth. He gave Adam detailed instructions of what to do with His creations. He later created the Garden of Eden for

Adam. Notice I did not say Eve, for she was not yet created. He then looked at Adam and said he needed a "help meet." He did not want Adam to be alone. So he then created Eve in the Garden of Eden. She was made to complete the first home. In Genesis 1:31 "And God saw everything that he had made, and, behold, it was good." This was the only perfect home. However, as we continue to read in Genesis we see that this home failed. Remember that God himself was Adam's father and walked with him daily, yet Adam failed as a husband and a father. Satan knew of the relationship between Adam and God and did not attack it. He tempted Eve not Adam. She fell prey and then passed her sin to Adam. Adam failed, not because of Eve but with Eve as his life partner. Adam failed as a husband because he failed to protect and lead Eve away from evil. Remember that it was Adam to whom God gave instructions. God wanted Adam to follow him, but Adam followed Eve (many men are still doing that today). Another thing to be aware of here is that just because God expelled Adam and Eve from Eden because of their sin does not mean that he does not want us to live in His blessings today. That is why he wrote down his recipe for an unbroken home in detail.

Being expelled from the Garden was the beginning, and it got worse from there. Adam also did not lead his sons properly as is evidenced by Cain and Able. But enough of pointing a finger at Adam and Eve. The point is that that Adam failed even though he and God fellowshipped daily. Where does that leave us? Because of Adam's failures, God began to divulge his plan to defeat Satan's attack against our homes; He wrote them in the Bible.

This recipe for healing is just that, a recipe. That means that it only tells us what <u>we</u> need to do; it does not do the work for us. Too often, we are looking for someone else to solve the problems that we are supposed to solve for ourselves. Laurie and I did that. We were blessed to have found Yvonne, a truly anointed and godly counselor that helped Laurie and me as we healed. Please be very careful of where you get your answers. If you need professional help in a particular area of your life, such as addiction, or mental health, you should seek a trained, Godly person for that need. This recipe is for people that want to stop blaming others, look into their own lives, , and determine to break some generational curses in their home. However, if your answers do not come from God's word, then they are man-made. One of the reasons for this book is because we did not find the answers we needed in the places we thought we should. What did happen is that we kept looking and praying and reading the Bible. What we discovered was that there is no one person or one book with all the answers except the word of God.

We found that true healing of brokeness is a growth process and does not happen all at once. That means it takes time, work, tears, and lots of faith. There is no magic bullet. We also found that Satan would go to unbelievable lengths to keep us from finding and staying in God's plan. This is a recipe that has to be applied day after day in order for it to work. Do whatever it takes to make it work for you and for future generations. By the way, you get as many "do-overs" as you want and you can go back to any part of the recipe as many times as you need. If you are anywhere as stubborn as I was, you will need to refer to it often to get it to stick.

Where do we start? You have to start from where you are today. It does not matter how bleak you may think that place is; you can get to where you want to be from there. Today is the beginning of the rest of your life. No matter how good life has or has not been for you, it can get better. If you are one of the fortunate few that have already unlocked this recipe and are living it daily, let your light shine for others to see. But start from where you are today. Even God cannot change history and tomorrow has not happened yet, so you have to start from where you are now.

With that being said, let's begin a journey that is going to amaze you. I am going to be brutally honest with you because that is what most of us need. I do not want to sound harsh or unforgiving, but your lives and the lives of your children and your children's children are at stake, so you need the truth. You are broken. Your parents were broken. Your children will be broken. You came from broken people that came from broken people etc.etc. Satan is in the business of brokeness and is at work 24/7 to break you and your home. There is no shame in being broken; brokeness makes you normal. He began in the Garden of Eden and he has not let up since. If you are reading this and your home is badly broken, you are in the right place. If you think that your home is not broken, keep reading and you will find that it can be better than ever. One of Satan's greatest tools is to make us believe that we are doing okay. There is no home that Satan does not attack and that Jesus cannot heal and protect. You will hear this many times before we are finished. Brokeness does not equate to failure and it is not final unless we surrender to the enemy. Too many people have surrendered much too young and are just waiting around for the long black car. By accepting our brokeness as unchangeable, we have surrendered our joy to the enemy. But today is the day that you can say, "Enough is enough"!

If you are married, you brought baggage (later to be identified as spirits) from two broken homes with you (by the truckload). If you are not married just follow along and you will have a head start on most people when your time comes. You will be able to intercept and avoid brokeness before you find that soul mate.

When you were married each of you thought that is was going to be "and they lived happily ever after" fairy tale. However, shortly after the honeymoon was over, reality happened. All his shortcomings became very apparent. All her imperfections were brought to light. She found out he snores and he found out she buys a lot of shoes. The fairy tale turned in to a war. (For some that is literal.) For Laurie and me, it was six months when the wheels fell off. For many, buyer's remorse sets in and the war begins. We have preconceived ideas as to what our home is going to be like, but we find, very quickly, that he or she does not fit the mold we had in our mind. We find ourselves living in a compromise or a war zone instead of a fairytale.

Well, let the healing begin. None of us are and never will be perfect. If we accept that "I" am not perfect and our spouse is not perfect and we stop trying to be or make them perfect, we can start down the road to healing. If you think you are perfect throw this book away now, you do not need it or God in your home. If you are trying to make your spouse perfect, then you are trying to be God and even he accepts that we are not perfect. Say this out loud right now "Neither I nor my spouse will ever be perfect on this earth."

Most of us think of broken homes as being riddled with abuse, alcoholism, poverty, drugs, and divorce. That is not always the case. Many homes are riddled with hidden pain. That hidden pain can lead to anger, depression, divorce, or even suicide. At the very least, it leaves someone unfulfilled and struggling. God did not create the home to be broken or "it's the best we can do" or "it's as good as I had it when I was growing up" or "it will get better someday." "That's the way my parents did it and that's good enough for me" does not cut it. And in Genesis He says, "He (man) will earn it by the sweat of his brow." In other words, it will not happen automatically just because you ask for it. Do not expect God to do what he has given you explicit instructions to do for yourself. God didn't break our homes, we did. You may think someone else broke your home, but that is not the case and we will deal with that in Chapter 3. What he will do is lead you to healing by his grace and mercy. One of the amazing things that happened to us is that, once we got past the pain, we found it to be exciting to grow in God's wisdom. It is actually fun to uncover his secrets and put them to work in our lives. The pain of failure will carry on for generations, but the joy of the Lord goes on forever!

If your children see you working against the things that break your home, they will learn from you and you will arm them for the war that will come against their homes. They will actually join you in your healing! If you don't work against the brokeness in your home, you will pass that brokeness on to them (just as I did). Exodus 20:5 "...I the Lord thy God am a jealous God, visiting the iniquity of the fathers upon the children unto the third and fourth generation of them that hate me"; I will give you a real life example of this in Chapter 3. So let's start today to pass these blessings on to the next generations!

NOTES

NOTES

THE SOURCE FOR HEALING

*T*HE next step in the healing process is to identify and accept the source of our healing. There was only one home ever created that wasn't broken and that home was perfect until the occupants decided to follow someone other than the Creator. (I hope that you have a very real relationship with Jesus, but if you don't today, you probably will before we are through.) Fortunately, Jesus will heal you if you just ask him, regardless of your present relationship with him. It was after he healed many people that they accepted him as their Savior. That's right, he will heal you before you accept him. In John 5: 8, 9 "Jesus saith unto him, Rise, take thy bed, and walk. And immediately the man was made whole..." Then in

John 5: 13 "And he that was healed wist not who it was…" This man did not know who Jesus was or who healed him or how He did it. Later Jesus revealed to him whom it was that healed him. Read John 5 for the whole story. In other words, sometimes, God will let us take him for a test drive just to show us how much he loves us and to show us what he can do for us. We need to accept the Bible as the truth. If you cannot accept this then you and your home are at the mercies of the "experts" of the world and many things that brings misery to us. Proverbs 1: 7 says, "The fear of the Lord is the beginning of knowledge; *but* fools despise wisdom and instruction."

We are born with a fear of falling and of loud noise. We are born with natural tendencies that are physical but without intelligence or respect. Everything after birth is learned. Some "learned" people disagree with that, but if you leave a baby in a room, treat it like a wild animal, and never let it see other people or the light of day you will end up with a dumb animal. So everything we know in our feeble little brains is what we have learned since birth.

The only major difference between animals and us is that God made us in THEIR own image (note multiple). Genesis 1: 26 "And God said, Let us make man in our own image, and after our likeness; and let them have dominion over the fish of the sea, and over the fowl of the air, and over all the earth…." (We will discuss "dominion" in detail in Chapter 4.) He gave us the ability to create thoughts and rule the earth with order. No other being was given the authority to think for themselves or to rule the earth. All other creatures were "programmed" by God to operate by instincts. You can teach a dog or many other animals tricks or to do what we want them to do, but they do not have a clue what they are doing. They just want the cookie. (We are like that sometimes.)

If God gave us the ability to think for ourselves, then he gave us the ability to understand and follow his instructions. Is there any other source in the universe other than his that works? The ones that are not of him are of the world and lead to failure and pain. Proverbs 5: 5 "Trust in the Lord in the all thine heart; and lean not unto thine own understanding." I am here to tell you that if I had understood this verse completely, I would have saved my family and myself a load of suffering!

When God created the universe, he put certain "laws" into place for our benefit. We cannot break any of these laws without consequences. Some of these laws are easy to understand and obey while others are not so easy. An easy example of God's law for us to understand is that of physics. Go up on the roof and jump. You will quickly prove the law of gravity. Put your hand in a fire and you will learn about heat energy. Those laws are presented in a way that cannot be avoided.

Spiritual laws are optional but have dire consequences if we disobey them and wonderful blessings if we do obey them.

These are the laws that we use to heal our homes. If man's laws worked, the courts would not be full of divorce cases and criminal prosecutions.

There are thousands of "brains" out there that believe they can out-think God. They shout out man-made ideas to sell you something that will not work. They write books, give lectures, and sell hundreds or DVD's. They are referred to in the Bible as false prophets. I tell you this because we bought into some of them. False prophets are those that want to give or sell us their ideas rather than help us learn and grow with God's word. They are usually easy to spot because they have their own agenda. Unfortunately, I know some pastors that fall into this category. This is an easy trap to fall into. Part of the recipe demands that you read the Bible on a regular basis for yourself. If you depend on human intelligence (including your own) for your guidance you are in for a fall.

Let me give you a simple example of God's wisdom verses man's wisdom. It took thousands of years, hundreds of lives and an untold amount of wealth for man to lift off the ground and soar 133 feet. It took a lot more deaths and trial and error before flight became a relatively safe and normal mode of transportation. God did it on day one before he even made Adam. We have no wisdom that compares to God's wisdom and never will. It is when we stop trying to out-think God that we will began to heal. That is the way it was for us too.

The purpose of this chapter is for you to understand that the only source that will heal you and your home is Jesus and his word. That being said, there are lots of books like this one that are testimonies of the results of studying the Bible and applying its wisdom that will help you in your growth process. Search for them and use them. God still uses ordinary people like you and me to spread and share his wonderful messages. God sent Laurie and me his word through several such "messengers."

SPIRITUAL LAWS

This is one of the spiritual laws God gave us; God does not allow for a vacuum. If we remove something from our being, then we must replace it with something else.

Don't let this next idea scare you. Our homes are broken because of the presence of "unclean" spirits sent by Satan. Those unclean spirits include selfishness, jealousy, pride, lust, hate, malice, disrespect and many more. Matthew 12: 43-45; "When the unclean spirit is gone out of a man, he walketh through dry places, seeking rest, and findeth none; Then he saith I will return into my house from whence I came out; and when he is come he findeth it empty, swept, and garnished. Then goeth he, and taketh with himself seven other spirits more wicked than himself, and they enter in and dwell there: and the last state of that man is worse than the first. Even so shall it be also unto this wicked generation.". (KJV) That means we must remove the things that break our homes, work continuously to keep them out, and replace them with things that heal and protect us. Later we will dig into how to do this.

If you are to begin to heal, you are going to have to accept some secrets that may be difficult to grasp. One of them is: YOU CANNOT CHANGE YOURSELF OR ANYONE ELSE! We do change, but it is from the inside out, not the other way around. You will only change by growth. Growth in others will have very little effect you. You must concentrate on your growth and healing and let others deal with their own.

How many times have we promised someone or had someone promise us, "I won't do that anymore?" That is someone trying to change from the outside. We cannot just change ourselves by promising ourselves or anyone else with words. We become frustrated with ourselves because, try as we may, we cannot change our behavior. Sometimes we just tell our loved ones, "That's just who I am, deal with it." Most of the time we just keep on going as we are and do not even realize anything is wrong. That is what my parents did with tragic results.

Healing is a matter of personal growth and that takes time. It is a slow process. If it were easy, anyone would do it. If we accept this first, it will prevent us from becoming frustrated with each other, God, and ourselves. Yes, you can and will become frustrated with God if you do not think He is giving you what you want, when you want it, and how you want it, or especially when he gives you answers that are painful. You can become frustrated with your spouse (as I did) if you think you are putting in more effort than they are or if you think they are dragging their feet. You can become frustrated with yourself if you become impatient. Some of us need more growth than others do. Some of us do not grow as fast as others do. Some of us (like me) are more stubborn.

The one promise we have is that Jesus said he would not forsake us and that he will be there with us every step of the way. If we could change ourselves, then we would not have any problems and we would not need God or his word.

An example of this replacement would be when we ask God to remove our selfishness. We would then have to learn how to sacrifice for others and put them ahead of ourselves. When we ask God to remove our sinful pride, we have to learn to be humble and serve others with joy and not resignation. I did not have a clue how to do those things. I had thought of only myself and my way for so long that I did not know how to think any other way. As you identify the areas in your life in which you need to grow, be patient with yourself, with each other, and with God. Regardless of how young or old you are, it took years for you to grow into the person you are today and it's going to take a while to grow out of that. And the only source we can trust for healing is the One that created us in the beginning.

The message here is that you can only choose to grow for yourself and not anyone else. The good news here is that if anyone in the home chooses to grow in God's word, then there is growth in that home. It is easy to use the excuse "I'll get started when he/she does his/her part." If you do that, you are letting Satan to continue to poison and destroy your home. Get started today on you regardless of your spouse or anyone else.

As I said before, you will have to read God's word for yourself to complete this recipe. I am not talking about just reading the Bible and expecting that to "fix" everything. I am saying we must accept that our answers for a joyful life are in the Bible, and then it is just a matter of finding them and putting them in play. Most of us just do not look for them, or just ignore the message when brought by others. All too often, we wait until the wheels fall off before we get started. You have to trust God and His word. We will help you find some of those answers that are in God's word in this book, but this book does not compare to the wisdom you will find in the Bible. The Bible is a living document for living people. When you read the Bible as living document from a living God, it becomes a spiritual experience. It has the answers to life and everything life brings. It has all the cures for Satan's poison and lies.

NOTES:

NOTES:

REMOVING THE BLAME

THE next step is probably going to be the most difficult to accomplish. I want you to remove one of the most devastating words ever written in any language from your vocabulary. That is the word "BLAME."

Webster's Dictionary says: **blame***: "1. to say or think that someone or something is the cause of what is wrong or bad 2. To find fault with; disapprove of; criticize".*

In later chapters, we will talk about accountability but, right now, let's deal with "blame."

I warned you in Chapter 1 that I was going to be brutally honest and here it comes. Blame is a smokescreen that we use to avoid the truth. No one, including God, is to blame for what has happened to us or to where events have taken us.

Now several people just threw this book in the trash or could not wait to send me their story about how wrong I am. Stay with me until I am finished, and if you can prove me wrong, I will rewrite this book on your behalf. (When the light of truth shines, it uncovers all things hidden in the dark.) When things go wrong, whether on the job, in the church, or in our homes, the first thing we do is to blame someone and that is exactly what the enemy wants us to do.

I know someone is typing an email to me to point out the child molester and how the innocent child was not to blame, or how he or she was abused and how the perpetrator is to "blame" and how the child is marked for life. Our court system (God help us) has even transferred the "blame" to abusive parents for the very person we were just talking about. Yes, the child molester wreaked havoc in the life of an innocent child, or the abuser in yours. This makes the child or you a victim. This makes the perpetrator accountable for his actions.

Please understand the difference between "blame" and accountability. What caused him to commit this tragedy is inside of him. I don't care what caused him to commit his crime, I want my family and you protected from him, and he is to be held accountable to the law, God's and man's. But, even if we stone him to death, the damage has been done.

Some may ask, "Why does God let this happen?" Do you realize to whom you are speaking? God is perfect (even if you question it) and cannot make any mistakes. Remember that there was no death or tragedy in the world until it became a place of sin and we are the sinners. There are millions of innocent victims throughout the earth, past and present. The news is full every day of stories of victims and perpetrators. But blame is a cancer inside of the person doing the blaming and just leads to more misery.

I hope that by the end of this chapter you deal with this terrible word. Blame intercepts God's healing power. He will deal with the perpetrator in his time. What he wants from you is to trust him without malice toward anyone or anything else so that he can minister to you. One of the saddest tragedies of mankind is when a selfish, evil person violates a totally innocent person and turns the victim into a miserable container of blame (hate) for life. Now we have two miserable and lost persons. The venom of selfish people has stung me many times in my life and not until I begged the Lord for healing did I realize how much of that venom I had kept inside of me for years.

Blame is the opposite of forgiveness. There is a prayer that says, "Forgive us our trespasses as we forgive others." According to this, our healing and forgiveness is conditional to our forgiveness of others. If you harbor any blame, you are actually telling God "I don't need your healing or forgiveness." This word handicapped our healing process for over a year! Blame is a ball and chain you let someone attach to your soul, give you the key, and then he or she just walks away. You can walk away from that ball and chain any time you wish. It may not be easy and it may take some work and prayer, but it can be done.

I would like to share some stories of tragedy, and how blame destroyed not only the life of the person doing the blaming but also destroyed others as well. The first story is about a home that was obviously broken. The oldest son left home at age 16. The second child, a son, took his own life at age 16. The youngest child, a daughter, married and left as quickly as she could in order to get out of the home. Although the parents were Christians, they did not deal with the tragedy of their son's death properly. Instead, they tried to find someone to blame. The son drove the family car into a cement bridge railing at close to 100mph. The father suggested that there was a mechanical failure and wanted to sue the manufacturer. This was only one of several attempts to "blame" someone for the failure that was obviously inside their home. The results were that the surviving children never got closure until years later. This tragedy haunted their home long after both parents passed away. The truth is this home was broken years before it was marred by suicide or rebellion and it could have been healed. I know because I am that oldest child.

This story is about a young couple that married shortly after graduating from high school. They were Salutatorian and Valedictorian of their graduating class and were madly in love with each other from the day they met. He was the apple of his family's eye. On a Sunday afternoon drive, a drunk driver crossed the centerline and hit them head on, killing all three. The drunk driver was supposed to be in jail serving weekends for a former DUI charge. The father of the innocent husband turned his anger into blame and total bitterness. He blamed a plethora of people including the court, the sheriff's department, and God. He slowly drank himself to death, even cursing God with his last breath. He destroyed the lives of his wife and eldest son with his "blame." His surviving son will not listen to the words of salvation to this day, not only him, but also his son's son. Now the grandson has two sons and the church and its word are off limits to two innocent children, all because of blame. He thinks that a church is a place for hypocrites to gather and fake each other out and the sad thing is that, most of the time, he is right. The reason he is right is that we try to hide our "blame" and sin from God. The real tragedy is not that the father died in his bitterness but that, so far, he has passed it on to three generations. (Remember Exodus 20:5) The innocent husband was my first cousin.

This was by far, the largest and most difficult hurdle Laurie and I had to overcome, and it will be for you as well. But, it is the key to your healing. Blame comes in so many disguises that it will be hard to recognize sometimes. It is so rooted in who we are that we have to work hard to identify and eliminate this poison from our homes. **Blame is the number one recipe for disaster in your home!** You <u>will not </u>heal if you leave that word in your vocabulary. You can replace blame with accountability and forgiveness and that is explained in Chapter 6. Millions of dollars and thousands of homes are thrown away every day in the name of blame.

I am going to come out and say this just as clearly as I can "Your spouse, God, nor anyone else is to blame for any of the brokeness of your home!" If everyone would just read and understand this chapter and then put this book down, we could save thousands of homes from pain and failure.

Blame is a direct result of selfishness. Blame is an excuse that we use to harbor bitterness against others. There I go again. Well, if you blame someone else you are telling him or her that he or she is responsible for your pain and you want him or her to fix it. That is not going to happen! You are also telling God "I want to keep this pain, I earned it, and I'm not going to let them get off that easy." You are responsible for your own healing and only God's recipe will do that, but it will not work if you hold onto your blame (bitterness). Go back right now and read very carefully the definition of "blame." If you resign yourself to the fact that the cause of your misery is someone else's doing, you have given him or her permission to make your life miserable indefinitely.

Blame is the excuse we use not to do our part to heal our home and ourselves. You can choose to be happy or carry around a bag full of blame or excuses. It is your choice. Blame leads to bitterness, bitterness leads to loneliness and loneliness leads to more blame.

The best description of how to deal with bitterness (blame) I have ever heard was from a woman that was testifying on a Christian radio station who had been raped and tortured. When asked how she had overcome the bitterness she replied, "I realized that bitterness is you drinking poison and expecting the other person to die."

The opposite of blame is forgiveness. Forgiveness is the business of God, and you must learn it from Him. Forgiveness is something you freely give not something you receive. We beg God for forgiveness but it is his to grant as a gift as he pleases. If you do not learn how to forgive, you will pass your bitterness on to others just as that father did. There is a right way to tell someone that they have hurt you but to blame others is going to hurt you even more.

I am not talking about the kind of forgiveness you ask for when you are caught with your hand in the cookie jar. The kind of forgiveness we are talking about here is what Jesus did on the cross. He gave his life to save the very ones that crucified him. Some of the very men that drove the nails into his body later recognized him as their savior and he loved them for it. That is the only kind of forgiveness that will erase blame out of your heart. The Bible says, "Hate sin, not people." When we do not separate the sin from the person, we are breaking God's law. This may be one of those things you need to discuss with your pastor to totally understand.

Use the note pages in the back of this book and carefully write down all the things you think are broken in your home or life today. Do not read any further until you have made your list. Later, you will uncover things you did not know were broken and to add to this list. Do not let anyone see your list. Husbands and wives should do this separately. You may choose to destroy it later at your leisure.

Got your list? Now put a mark by any of them that require change on someone else's part. Be honest here.

Now, write a new list that requires only the changes you need to make. Many of you will have very little on your second list. The difference between the first and second list is blame. That wasn't fair, was it? But that is how basic blame is and how Satan uses it against us.

Now let's say that God says "I want you to solve these things on your own without putting any responsibility on anyone else, and you can get all the help you want from anywhere you wish". Where would you begin? When it became apparent in the Old Testament that we could not obey God's law and that if judged by the law, we were all going to burn in hell, God took it upon himself to give us a solution to our problem. If he were to "blame" us for our sins and hold us accountable (which He will do someday), we would all burn for eternity. Instead, he gave us someone to take our punishment for us and to remove any "blame" he may have against us.

Back to your list. Now write out for each problem what you can do about it. If you admit you do not have the answers for some of these things, you are on the right track. That is the reason for this book. Save these lists for later as you will be adding the things from which you want to be healed and marking off things for which you have found the solution and healing. <u>Do not</u> share your lists with anyone until you have a witness of complete healing. Down the road of healing, you may want to acquire an accountability partner of the same sex that you trust (not your spouse). I highly recommend that you do. You may share your lists with them but only if you have built a complete faith in their walk and integrity. Be careful; this isn't a pity party!

The examples of blame that I gave you are extreme. Let's look at some other examples that you may find in your home that are not so extreme. Let's say you have a son that is old enough to be out of diapers. His personality begins to present itself and he does something that needs correction or discipline. One of you makes the comment; "He is just like his father" or "he got that from your side of the family." Sounds innocent enough doesn't it.

What did the child really hear? If I do something my parents do not like, it is their fault (blame). Or, it's my grandparent's fault. You are saying that someone else had something to do with the child's misbehavior as well as losing a chance to teach accountability. That is how basic blame can be. Will we stand before God and say, "My sin is my parent's fault"? Will God say "That's ok, it was the way you were raised"?

Raising two sons through the teenage years (without any prior training on my part) taught me some things. When there was evidence that someone had broken the rules, (i.e.: broken glass on the floor, notes from school, calls from neighbors, etc.) they would invariably blame the other or someone else. Where did they get that? They got it from the world, including their parents and everyone else around them. That is what Adam and Eve did. "It was the serpent's fault." Adam even blamed Eve to God's own face. This is natural human behavior and it only means we are normal. If your conversations about anything in the home are about who or what caused it rather than what we can do about it, you are wasting a lot of time and words.

Start listening, and I mean really listening, to you. I did not say to others, I said to you. Do not keep an account of what others say, just pay attention to what you speak. When Laurie and I started doing that, things began to change in a hurry.

The Bible says, "The tongue is a sword." That simply stated means the tongue is a lethal weapon. It means that we actually can and do speak brokeness into our homes and can speak healing also. I hope that you understand just how deadly the tongue can be when used to place blame. It is the most deadly poison you can bring into your home.

Please remember that you are addressing something that has been going on from the beginning of time. Be patient as this is going to take some time to deal with properly. You are going to need to come back to this chapter again and again to get to where you want to be.

NOTES

NOTES

NOTES

Your Four Walls

FOUR WALLS

There is only one place that God's spiritual laws were intended for use to defeat the enemy on a daily basis. Of all the things I learned from the Bible, this is the most powerful message I have ever learned. This is going to require that you accept a simple spiritual truth. The idea of "four walls" is found in Genesis, when " God said....let them have dominion

....over all the earth." Dominion means "the power of governing or rule." In other words, God gave us the right to rule our world and that "world" is our home. God did not take away our dominion of the world Just because we fell into sin. This is still true today. Though it is hard to believe, he gave you and I complete dominion (rule) of our home. Let this sink in deep: you are going to experience all of your growth and healing from inside your home, not at church, the counselors, a bible study, a group meeting or anywhere else. That is where the healing is needed and that is where Jesus will come and minister to you. Satan wants us to look anywhere else but there because that is where he attacks us. You will get information and knowledge and support from the other outside sources, but your healing can and will happen only in your home because that is where you live and have dominion. The reason that we had to deal with "blame" first is because we would use it to give up that power. This step in the recipe is to reclaim and accept the power to defeat Satan in our lives and homes.

Take a blank sheet of paper and draw a square in the center. Make your square large enough to write some things inside of it. Now draw two stick people inside the square (one if you are single). Now keep that picture where you can glance at it from time to time. That picture represents your "dominion". In Genesis 2: 24 God said "Therefore shall a man leave his father and mother, and shall cleave unto his wife; and they shall be one flesh." If you are married (or are living with someone) your dominion includes both people. If you have children they are temporary residents, and they are there to learn from you how to run their homes when their time comes. Now you may not yet understand how much power you have, but you actually have complete control of all the spirits that enter those four walls. Again, stop for a moment and let that sink in. It may be difficult for you to accept right now, but it's in the Bible. That is not to say that all those spirits are welcome, or if you expel them they stay gone. If I lost you for a moment, don't worry, you will get it. Our healing is a matter of determining which spirits we want inside of those walls and understanding what to do about them and how to deal with the ones we do not want there.

Most of us do not even realize what spirits have found their way into our home and lives or where they came from. They actually reside inside of us and go everywhere we go. Many of us have resigned ourselves just to put up with them. How sad. Others just ditch the whole home, blame the other person, file for divorce, and start over, and over, and over. It is imperative that you accept that you can take back this power in your home. We will share how to wield that power to defeat Satan as we go along, but God gave it to you and it is yours unless you <u>willingly</u> give it up. If you give up that power, you give up your true freedom. (I hope I just heard someone stand up and shout for joy.)

Let's not confuse spirits with feelings. Feelings include happiness, excitement, peace, sorrow, resentment, sadness, loneliness, anger, jubilation, confusion, disappointment, abandonment, and many others. Feelings happen inside of us because of something that happened outside of us. A spirit is something we choose from the inside with which to conduct ourselves and deal with things outside of us.

Most of the time our feelings are a reaction to spirits that have invaded our four walls. An example of feelings is when something good happens, like winning a game, having a new baby, or having him pop the big question or having her say, "Yes". Before she says yes or before we hear that healthy cry, we are full of anxiety and fear. Her answer determines his next feeling. That cry determines our next feeling. There are many things that bring bad feelings such as an insult, rejection, ridicule, tragedy, and oppression just to name a few. No matter what feelings we experience, something causes them. It's easy to share the good feelings, but what about the bad ones? The first reaction to bad feelings is to look for the cause of the feeling and go into the attack mode. We have already identified this in Chapter 3, and it's called blame. That is exactly what Satan wants you to do. God wants you to identify the spirit and attack **it**, not the person that brought it. This is where we get to choose good spirits. Unfortunately, we humans have a bad habit of holding onto our hurt (blame) for years. I told you this was not going to be easy, and it just got a lot more difficult. We cannot always control our feelings but we can control what we do about them. Jesus had feelings, one of which was sorrow. The shortest verse in the Bible is John 11:35 "Jesus wept." His sorrow was for his friend Lazarus who had died. God gave us feelings to help us identify the spirits at work in our lives. Then he gave us this recipe and the example of what to do about it. The hard part is that we have been the way we are for many years and habits that entrenched are difficult to deal with. You can and will find a wonderful new life with this power and with some work.

This happened as I was writing this book. On Sunday February 19, 2012, Laurie and I received a text while in church to get to the hospital as soon as possible. Our daughter-in-law was due with our eighth grandchild and she was about to deliver. We got to the hospital and found that they had just rushed her into surgery for an emergency c-section. We waited outside the delivery area with my son and granddaughter with great anticipation. A short while later the nurse came out to inform us that my son's wife was fine but the baby boy did not make it. A little while later, I cried and my heart broke as I held an otherwise perfect, but lifeless, child in my arms, and had to deal with a pain that no one should ever have to endure. Now I could have "blamed" God, the doctor, the hospital or anything else I chose. However, by the mercy and grace of Jesus Christ I could close my eyes and could see our Joey on Jesus' lap. It did not make my pain go away and it still hurts, but I did not add the pain of selfish blame as I did at my brother's death. I shared this with you to tell you that it is your choice to turn your feelings of pain and sorrow into a blessing or something else. Your relationship with Jesus will determine that choice. Our family will heal and the pain will subside as long as we do not get in the way of God's healing and blessings.

The next step is to identify these spirits and determine how to deal with them. These spirits include pride, selfishness, jealousy, lust, anger, hate, greed, fear, love, sacrifice, humility, love, praise, compassion, and kindness, just to name a few. As you identify all those spirits that are present in your home today, good or bad, write them on the inside of the square you drew. Be honest and do not just write the good ones. Notice that some of these spirits and feelings have the same name. It will take some work and study to understand the difference between a feeling and a spirit. But, remember this, for every evil spirit there is a good spirit to replace it and it is as a matter of choice.

It would be nice in today's world to have a remote control to bring up a menu and turn on the spirits we want and turn off the ones we do not want. The reality of life is that Satan is throwing every evil spirit in his arsenal at you and your home constantly, and God's good spirits have to be searched for and manually inserted. Understand also that you may win a battle against a spirit today and loose against that same spirit tomorrow. This is an ongoing war until the day we leave this earth.

A word of warning here; the only spirits you have dominion over are the ones in you, so only write down the spirits you want removed from you. If you write spirits that you have identified in others, then you need to make a new list, which is a prayer list. You can only attack those spirits with prayer and faith. That means that you cannot do anything about the spirits in others except take them to Jesus in prayer and this includes the spirits in your spouse. This is one of the spiritual laws that God wrote in His book and you cannot change it. Chapter 5 addresses the tools you will need to deal with these spirits.

Many people marvel when they hear that someone was miraculously cured of some terrible disease or medical condition. I wish every sick person in the world were healed today. If I were sick in my body and became healed by a miracle, I would tell everyone. That being said let me tell you about and even greater miracle. These bodies we inhabit are temporary. Some day we are going to dispose of them and move on. Therefore, any healing of this body is also only temporary. The real miracle of healing our spirit is something that is going to last for eternity. The healing that this recipe brings is about a healing of the soul that will affect generations to come. The healing of physical infirmity pales compared to the healing of the wounds Satan inflicts to our souls. The healing that Laurie and I receive still astounds us every day.

Let us share with you some of our story and how this recipe worked for us. You must hear the depth of our brokeness for you to understand how miraculous God's recipe is.

I married a week after my high school graduation in 1969. We had two sons born in 1972 and 1974. Our marriage was a disaster. Oh, there were some fun times and some good memories, but it finally ended in separation and divorce 37 years later. We never got it right. After three years of single life, I met Laurie. She had been married 3 times. . We actually met in a bar/restaurant on October 7, 2008. (I <u>do not</u> recommend that anyone go looking for your soul mate in a bar!) Two weeks into our courtship, the Holy Spirit stepped in and called us and we accepted Christ. (I thought I had accepted Christ in 1970, but I didn't follow through with him.) We were baptized together in February 2009. After a six-month romance, we were married in April 2009. She is the most beautiful and alluring woman I have ever met.

A few months after the honeymoon, cracks began to appear in our relationship. We had gone to premarital counseling, attended church every Sunday, and were trying to stay on track. It did not work. I made her a trophy and turned her into an idol and a sex object. She began to resent me, which turned into pure hatred. She had sustained a serious back injury while serving in the military and was under heavy medication for pain and depression. We began to question these medications and found that she was being over medicated. (We are not placing "blame" here.) The fact is that several doctors were treating her simultaneously and her medication was uncoordinated. Without her realizing it, she had become addicted to prescription drugs for 10 years! In addition to powerful pain and muscle relaxers, she was on heavy anti-depressants. We found a doctor that helped us with a detoxification process. She came out from under the influence of the drugs six months later only to find herself married to someone she hardly knew and didn't like (she actually hated every man in the world and I was target number one). She also had to deal with the pain of a divorce in 2005 and the loss of the only mother figure she ever knew (her grandmother) in 2008, and now was remarried. I found myself in a phone booth with a wild animal.

It got worse before it got better. She had been chemically leveled (emotionally) for ten years. After several months of counseling, we began dealing with the fact that Laurie had been abused and rejected her whole life. Her mother had given custodial rights of Laurie to her grandmother when Laurie was just a baby. When she was twelve, she learned she was an illegitimate child from an extramarital affair. The man she called father had divorced her mother because of that affair and holds that against Laurie to this day. Then an older man that took the position of a father figure sexually abused and raped her through manipulation when she was sixteen. She married at nineteen and divorced eleven months later when the abuse became physical. She married again at age 27 and divorced six months later when she learned that he was a pathological liar. She married a third time at age 32 and this lasted 5 years until she could not take his verbal abuse any longer.

So God took a badly abused woman and put her in a home with a selfish sexual delinquent. Go figure.

I had been raised in a home that was basically full of selfishness, and I am telling you that I was a very self-centered, selfish person. Furthermore, I was an arrogant know-it-all that would not listen to anyone except myself. For more than a year, I could not touch her or even get near her without her tensing up in pain. Many times, sometimes almost daily, her pain erupted into fierce anger. Now, if God's recipe could fix this mess, and he did, he will not have any problem with yours. We found our four walls full of pain and blame. One by one, we began to identify the "spirits" that had put the pain in us, and started looking for ways to eliminate them. One of the secrets to getting things out of your four walls is to understand that you can ask Jesus to help, and that he is the only power that can make that happen. Laurie could not eliminate my selfishness and I could not deal with her pain and anger. It took two years for us to realize the miracle of God's healing power.

Today we enjoy a wonderful marriage full of love and respect thanks to this recipe. We have shared this recipe with several others and they are amazed at what is happening in their lives as well.

We will discuss how to do this shortly, but right now, you need to understand that I could only work on me and she on herself, but we could and did help each other. This also means that you have to give the other(s) inside your walls the room and support to grow. This can be hard to do. To do this you have to take everything, especially the negative, to Jesus. Again, be patient with each other. All you need to know now is that you have the power and the source to deal with all the spirits inside your four walls.

NOTES

NOTES

Identifying the Enemy

L ET's go to work inside your four walls. This is where the real work begins. This step requires you to be honest with God and yourself. Genesis 2:25 says "And they were both naked, the man and his wife, and were not ashamed." The perfect home was still intact at this time and sin had not entered yet. So there was no reason to hide anything from God or each other. God's recipe requires us to expose ourselves completely to him. This is a major stumbling block for most of us, especially the men. All of the integrity within your home is a result of your personal honesty with God, and it will be forever. This is where the men have to take the lead. It is the man that God appointed the priest of the home. It is important that husband and wife both do this, and the recipe will not work unless they both eventually do this. Here's the good news; this will set you free! When Jesus cast the demons into the pigs it set the possessed man free just as it will us.

If you went to the doctor with symptoms that alarmed you, would you try to hide some of them? Suppose the diagnosis was serious but curable. Would you follow the doctor's advice? If you were told that if you ignored the treatment you would become completely disabled and live the rest of your life in pain and misery, what would you do?

The recipe in the Bible demands that you give God access to all the broken things that need to be healed. Mark 7: 21-23 "For from within, out of the heart of men, proceed evil thought, adulteries, fornications, murder, thefts, covetousness, wickedness, deceit, lasciviousness, an evil eye, blasphemy, pride, foolishness; All these evil things come from within, and defile the man." These are the things that Jesus helps us deal with. He would rather heal us than judge us and we leave him no choice but to do one or the other. You will find out how badly that he wants to heal you in Chapter 6.

Throughout the New Testament, you will find examples of Jesus and the disciples traveling about and "casting out spirits and healing many." Notice that Jesus and his disciples did not destroy these spirits or remove them from the world. They "cast" them out of the person to some other place. These spirits will not be destroyed until they and the lost are cast into the eternal fire as told in Revelations. We need to realize that the spirits they cast out 2000 years ago are the same spirits we are dealing with today and they will always be in the earth. And remember, just because you cast a spirit out for the moment does not mean it will not come back, sometimes in a matter of minutes.

I know how difficult it was for me to accept that I had brought some really evil spirits into our relationship, and it is not going to be easy for you. This is where you need real honesty from yourself. Proverbs 25:28 "He that hath no rule over his own spirit is like a city that is broken down, and without walls." That means that when we hide or fail to be honest with God we have no rule over our own spirit and that leaves us exposed to all of the enemy's demons. No one likes to go looking for his or her defects. The spiritual truth is that our defects are sinful spirits that invade us and causes behavior that we do not want by turning us into someone we do not want to be. Where did they come from? They have been here since the Garden of Eden. We have been passing them down from one generation to another from the beginning and God does not want us to keep doing that.

Let me give an example of a spirit of anger and how it is passed along. I am driving with one of my grandchildren in the back seat. A driver cuts me off and puts us all in danger. Instead of getting angry, I just say "Whoa dude. That was close. He really needs to pay attention to what he's doing." Another time, my grandson is riding with someone else, the same thing happens, and that driver gets angry and curses the other driver. Now my grandson has two examples from which to choose for himself. Many times our children do not get that first choice.

The sad fact is that we do not think we are wrong when we lash out when we have been hurt. We justify it with "Well, he was wrong and he almost killed us!" Be honest, how many angry words find their way into your home? There is something called righteous anger that is explained in many places in the Bible. Right now, we are talking about the spirit of unhealthy anger, and how it finds its way from one generation to another. I could write a huge book on the times I let my anger rule me instead of me ruling it. Most of us could. Did it ever occur to you that the person or object you are angry at doesn't care? Many times, the other person wants you to be angry. If that's the case, they won.

I made a covenant with God when I met Laurie that if he would help me stop from ever saying anything in anger to intentionally hurt her, that I would do my best to follow his word for the rest of my life. He has done just that, so here I am. There is a way to properly deal with contention but anger is not it.

The most powerful evil spirit is pride. Pride was the very first sin and it happened, because of selfishness, in heaven and not on earth. It is pride that stops us from being transparent before God and ourselves. God is in the "healing business" but he will not let you hold onto things that compromise His medicine (word). You may be praying with all your heart for your marriage or home and God is saying, "Ok, bring me **all** your broken parts and I will deal with them in the order that will heal you." For most of us, the number one block is pride.

The opposite of pride is humility. Jesus was the most humble, but yet powerful person that ever lived. Moses wrote much of the Old Testament and led Israel to the Promised Land, and was the most humble man alive at the time. How do we replace pride with humility? We begin by looking for ways to first serve Christ first and then serve others. If you serve in a way that draws attention to what you have done for your glory, then it is done in a prideful spirit and holds no true value.

I love to find ways to do things for Laurie and my family that they do not even know about. Some of these things are so simple, but yet say so much like: Men, get up early one Saturday and do the laundry, wash the dishes and sneak out the door before your golf game. When asked about it, gaff it off. Women, go for one week without criticizing him in any way and give him at least one or two compliments. Start reading your Bible in private when no one else is around looking for answers to help you be what God wants you to be. Start praying for people that have wronged you and have made themselves an enemy. Can you imagine a home where everyone works and looks for ways to make the others' lives as good as can be?

Pride will completely destroy your Christian witness. I know that we all want to help others with their walk, but pride will turn our witness into judgment. Proverbs 29:3 says: "A man's pride shall bring him low: but honor shall uphold the humble spirit." This means that the same words spoken by a man of pride carry no weight as when they are spoken by a humble man. Again, be patient with yourself. Read in the book of Proverbs every day and you will be amazed at how many times the wisest man that ever lived, (except Jesus) Solomon, talks about pride. If you feel you have a problem with pride, and most of us do, try this. There are 31 chapters in the book of Proverbs. Read one chapter each day for a year. That means you will read the book of Proverbs 12 times in the next year. I did that to help conquer my pride problem and it works (I still read it every day). Pride breaks a person from the inside out. Over and over, the Bible says, "pride comes before a fall." It was pride that started our spiritual war in heaven.

How many of you men would want a wife that respects and adores you? How many of you women want a man that loves you so much that he just looks for ways to make you happy and secure? The main thing that keeps that from happening is pride. True love is without pride. One of the traps as you grow is to think, "Ok God, I've got it from here." To stop studying and growing in God's word is like jumping out of an airplane with a parachute, getting half way to the ground and start cutting the cords and saying "It's ok, I can take it from here." That is what your prideful spirit will do. Satan will let you think that you can do it on your own and that is pure pride and a recipe for disaster. God is in the love business, not in the crisis management business. We cut the cords and then start crying out when we fall. This recipe is about letting him help you before it becomes a disaster. You would not want a friend that only shows up when they need something from you, so why do we treat God like that?

Good enough for man is not good enough for God. A humble spirit takes time to grow and is an ongoing project. If you are trying to grow or change to suit your spouse or any other human, you should quit right now, go get a beer and watch TV. This is another hidden spiritual law: You should play for an audience of one and that one is Jesus. The trap here is that you might resign yourself to follow this recipe just enough to get by. If that is the case, you are probably reading this just to get someone off your back. Stop now! Don't do that. You are lying to yourself and to them. Sorry, have to be real here. You have to go all-in just like Jesus did to save us and like Satan does to destroy us.

Another spiritual law is the planting of seeds. Just like everything else God designed, we plant a seed, nurture it and protect it until it becomes mature in our nature. The seed we want to plant is humility. You will have to work at it with your will because our pride is natural and humility is unnatural. True humility is not "giving of one's self," it is "giving your whole being" or sacrificing yourself completely for something greater than yourself. One of the greatest things we have found was that the more humble we are the faster we grow. Pride allows the enemy to trap the spirits inside us we do not want. It will take some work on your part to identify the many evil spirits Satan uses, but the recipe for healing is the same for each and pride will stop God's access to the root of the problem.

One of the "soul-moles" he uses against men is lust. If we are not taught at a young age about our sexual nature, our bodies, and the world will lead us on down the road in ignorance. Teenage birth rates clearly tell us how we are doing with this one. Time to be honest men! The reason we do not do a good job here is that we find it easier to go along with the world's way instead of God's way.

Pornography and sexual sin has destroyed more homes than we even know about. It is the "closet" sin. If you think a little sneak look here or there or an innocent peak in a magazine is harmless, think again. God is a just God. What if he says he is going to allow the same access to your wives or daughters that you take with other women with your eyes and mind? Would you change anything? I know a man that lost the job of a lifetime by misuse of the company computer on porn sites. He devastated his family with his lust and weakness. When Satan attacks with this one, he has the advantage. Our TV's, billboards and magazines are full of ads using sex to sell their goods and it works because we look. The deck is stacked against us men.

I know about this one personally because I was addicted to sex. When our counselor called me out on it, I got mad and stormed out of her office. After months of battling inside myself, I went back and confessed she was right. The good news is that I decided to fight and today it is behind me, but I still have to be on guard for Satan's traps in this area. There is a great book by Tim Alan Gardner named "Sacred Sex" and another book by Kenny Luck named "Every Man's God's Man" that will help you conquer this demon. Men, if you do not have a Christian accountability partner, start looking for one,. You will probably need one to help in this area, or you may even need professional counseling. This has become an epidemic in our society, but it can be conquered.

If we fathers do not know how to conduct ourselves, then who is going to teach our sons and daughters? I was amazed as God began dealing with me in this area. In Matthew 6:22, 23 Jesus says "The light of the body is the eye: if therefore thine eye be single, thy whole body shall be full of light. But if thine eye be evil, thy whole body shall be full of darkness. If therefore the light is in thee be darkness, how great is that darkness." When Peter stepped out of the boat and onto the water, he was fine until he took his eye off Jesus. He began to sink when he put his eye anywhere except on Him. There is no other place as far away from God as a lustful eye.

I hate to have to admit this, but I began to watch the eyes of men in my church during worship service and it is shameful. If you look at any woman with a lustful eye, whether on the computer, TV, magazine, street, or anywhere you are making all women (including your wife and daughters) sex objects. In its purest form, that makes you a predator. Read Proverbs Chapter 5. This has become an epidemic in our society and it is time we brought it out in the open and stand up against it with integrity and honesty.

In my younger years I attended a party where there was an old 8mm projector and the guy hosting the party gave me my first exposure to pornographic film. Years later, he was horrified when viewing pornography on the Internet and found that the star of the film he was watching was his daughter. This is not an easy battle. It took me over a year to know that we had defeated this spirit in our home. (I told you before that I was stubborn!) Now, I am blessed to be able to help others that are very dear to me fight the same battle.

It is the men that must take the lead in this area. The results of our neglect here results with sons that think sexual conquests are going to make them a man and daughters that give up their most precious gift to get love they didn't get at home. That may seem a little harsh, but that's the way it is. You do not have to take my word for it, just look around in your own neighborhood.

Men, there is no integrity in your home unless you put it there. We all want respect from our wives and peers but too often do very little to build the character that will make that happen. When presented with a lustful temptation we have less than 3 seconds to have a victory or a defeat. We can carry that on further to everyday decisions, especially those in the home. Many decisions we have to make, as men, require us to choose between character and comfort. That is explained very well in "Every Man's God's Man."

It is never too late to start putting integrity into our homes. If you have not seen the movie "Courageous," go get it and watch it. The book "The Resolution" from the movie is also a wonderful growth study.

A wise man once said , "Show me the books a man reads and I'll tell you his character." Another put it this way, garbage in-garbage out. You can fall in love with the man in the mirror with just a little work. Build yourself a library of books such as we have mentioned here. Develop a reading habit that includes them and, most importantly, the Bible.

A wise old Indian was sitting under the shade of a tree talking with his grandson one sunny afternoon. His grandson was asking questions about life. He asked, "Grandfather, why is it I sometimes do things that I know are wrong but I do them anyway?" The wise old man said, "Grandson, there are two wolves inside of you fighting for control of you. A good wolf and a bad wolf." "Grandfather, which one wins?" In his wisdom his grandfather said, "Grandson, the one you feed." How often do you feed your good wolf?

The most difficult spirit for a woman to deal with is respect. I Ephesians 5:33 Paul wrote "Nevertheless let every one of you in particular so love his wife even as himself; and the wife reverence her husband." The Bible spends and extraordinary amount of words to instruct men about their behavior but not as much to the wives. The reason for this is that God wants the men to take the lead.

I know many wives are thinking, "here comes that submit thing." The real meaning of this part of the Bible is about honor, not submission. Jimmy Evans has written books and preached many sermons about this. His message is simple: A wife is to honor her husband, no matter what, and a husband is to love his wife, no matter what. If the wife just sits back and waits for him to show her love before she shows him honor, she will never succeed. Disrespect to the husband will open him and the marriage to all kinds of lethal spirits.

It is a man's nature to slay the dragon or conquer the enemy. (If you don't understand what a man's heart is about, go get the book "Wild at Heart" and start reading.) If his reward for his battle and wounds is criticism or being ignored, why should he seek the pain of growing and going to battle for you?

Without the patience and prayers of my wife, we would still be mired in the muck of my lust and pride. Proverbs 23: 7 says, "For as he thinketh in his heart, so is he:" Nothing goes into a man's heart any deeper or faster than the words of his wife. If you continuously tell him how disappointed you are in him or how he falls short of your expectations, he is going to live up to your words. Our spouses are a gift from God and many women are very disappointed after they unwrap theirs. You do not want to disrespect him just because he is not perfect, as that will just add more failure to the home where you want peace and love. That is absolutely against God's word and recipe for your home.

I have a friend who confided in me recently that he could not take it anymore. He loves his wife and children but he has come to the conclusion that he will never live up to her expectations and it is futile to even try anymore. His home may be about to endure the ultimate failure because of disrespect. Even if it survives, it is going to be a painful place until they grow out of that. I am not pointing the finger at her as she is a Godly woman and loves her children, but she has set the bar of respect so high that it does not allow him to be a man or the room to grow into that man. He says that no matter how much he tries it is never enough. He feels defeated.

This is difficult for women because they have to show respect to an imperfect man. I have news for you: the only perfect man was nailed to a cross 2000 years ago! The closest thing you will find to a "perfect" man is one who is on his knees daily trying to learn and grow in God's word, and these days that is a rare and wonderful thing.

If he is not that man yet, start speaking to him as if he already is, and see what happens. If you have not already heard me let me get this straight for you; his number one need from you is **not** sex, it is honor (respect). If a man thinks his is going to get accolades from you, he will try to conquer the world for you! When my wife realized the strides Jesus was making in our home, she went from a woman that hated all men (especially me) to witnessing before a group of women about the man God put in her life. (Remember that every man in her world had abused her for 41 years including me!) And the day she looked me in the eye and said, "I am so proud of you" my world became complete. There is no turning back for me! It is worth every tear and pain.

Regardless of how you use your power over your man, he will be exactly what you speak him to be. I do not believe any woman wants to be married to a "sorry" man. He will only be as "sorry" as you tell him he is. Warning! Too many men demand that respect or go looking outside their home with tragic results! This is not an excuse that you men can use the old cliché "If I don't get it at home then…" Men, it is your duty to honor your vows regardless of whether or not you get respect at home. And if you demand respect from your wife you will have a very empty victory.

Women, it is your job, and you have the power, to help protect him from falling and filling that void somewhere else. This is a major part of the recipe and like any other recipe, if you leave out any of the key ingredients, you will not like the results. Get the book "Love and Respect" to really get a handle on this one.

When I began my battle with my sexuality and my selfishness, I went to Laurie and asked her to be patient with me and help me while I was healing (growing). It was amazing. She became my number one cheerleader and walked by my side through it all. If she had stood across the room pointing her finger at me, we would have gotten nowhere. The Bible says in Matthew 18:20 "For where two or three are gathered together in my name, there I am in the midst of them." Well, in order to get these spirits out of your home, the two of you have to stand against them together. Remember in Chapter 1 about a place of "peace and harmony and without strife"? Women, if you do not hear anything else in this book please hear this: If you speak to or about your husband in any manner without respect, according to the Bible, you are poisoning your marriage.

Proverbs 12:4 "A virtuous woman is a crown to her husband; but she that maketh ashamed is as rottenness in his bones." Proverbs 14:1 "Every wise woman buildeth her house: but the foolish plucketh it down with her own hands (words)." (KJV) If you are having trouble understanding this go back and read the definition of blame again and get that book "Love and Respect".

No man can make a woman show respect, but he can do the things that will help him to earn it. It only happens because a woman chooses to do it of her own free will. Remember that this is God's recipe and if you disagree, you need to take it up with Him. As I stated earlier, listen, really listen to your words as they speak of the spirit that is in control of your heart at the moment.

Remember the lists you each made in Chapter 2? Go back to the list (be honest now) and add any of the things we have spoke about in this chapter. If there is any man out there that has not let his thoughts or his eyes go to unhealthy places I would like to meet him. If there is any woman out there that has never spoken with disrespect to or about her husband, I would like to meet her. If there is anyone out there that has never turned his or her pain into anger and/ or blame, please go get some forgiveness right now for your lie.

As I stated earlier, this is an ongoing battle and Satan will trick you again and again. We are just human. That is why we need God's recipe over and over to heal and protect our homes.

Here is a secret Satan does not want you to understand: The door that lets all evil spirits into our home is selfishness. It is this spirit that triggers pride, lust, jealousy, anger, disrespect and all the other evil spirits. Without selfishness, those other evil spirits have no support.

Picture a row of potted plants, each one representing an evil spirit. The soil and fertilizer around the roots that causes them to grow is selfishness. If our thoughts are centered on God and others, we put a chokehold on all the evil spirits.

There is a lab available to learn all we need to know about selfishness. All you have to do is watch everyone around us (including ourselves). Selfishness is something we learn from day one of life. Let a baby get hungry and you will see what I mean. They will let you know in a loud voice they want something from you and they want it now. Watch kids playing or adults when they do business.

My profession for 45 years has taken me in and out of homes and businesses daily. You would be amazed at some of the things I have seen and heard. I have seen a lot of loving and peaceful homes. I have also been in some that I could not wait to get away from. All of the broken homes (including my own) had one thing in common: selfishness. Alcohol, drugs, affairs, homosexuality, contention, anger, pride are all the results of selfishness. They are the causes of a broken home but its selfishness that brings them in and allows them to take root in our homes. It is deeply woven into our culture. So how do we root out something so natural and so deep? We have to grow out of it. Study the Bible and learn how to sacrifice for others the same way Jesus did for you. The loneliest place on earth is a house occupied by two or more selfish people. This was the atmosphere that led to my brother's suicide and the failure of the home where I grew up, and it had two parents that loved us to the best of their ability.

Sometimes all it takes is one person to decide to change and the cycle can be broken. Can you imagine what would happen if all parties decided to put an end to it and go "all in"? It starts with a decision and a commitment. Remember that it does not matter which one brings the spirit inside the four walls, it is deadly poison for everyone there. The only medicine we have for the other's selfishness is forgiveness, patience and prayer and make our life an example of giving. And you may ask, "What if they continue to be selfish over and over." You forgive them over and over. You pray for them over and over. This recipe is for all the people inside your four walls but only if they accept it. If you are trying to address someone else's evil spirits, all you can do is pray and bring your faith against those spirits. You have to trust God and wait for him to answer your prayers. It just got a little harder didn't it?

Another evil spirit that can damage your home is jealousy. The jealousy I am talking about is not the simple jealousy of toys or earthly objects. Those are fleeting thoughts that usually pass quickly. I am talking about a jealousy of love inside the home. I am talking about a deep-rooted jealousy that turns into resentment and anger.

God tells us that He is a jealous God. Mark 12:30,31 says, "And thou shalt love the Lord thy God with all thy heart, and with all thy soul, and with all thy strength: this is the first commandment. And the second is like, namely this, Thou shalt love thy neighbor as thyself. There is none other commandment greater than these." (KJV) Jesus is saying that unless we follow these commandments first, we are headed down the wrong road. It is selfish jealousy when we withhold or modify our love because we do not believe the other person is worthy of it or has earned it. How do you think God felt when Adam failed? I am sure his heart was broken but he did not stop loving him just because he failed. This is a difficult spirit to manage because our feelings get in the way.

Let's bring this into the home. If either spouse is not seeking to meet the needs of the other, there will be a natural jealousy. This can be good or bad depending on how we deal with it. God wants you to take it in a good direction while Satan wants the opposite.

Let me give you a life example. When Laurie was diagnosed with PTSD (post-traumatic stress disorder) and after she was free from the drugs, we began our painful and slow healing process. I was angry with the people that had abused her and put her in such a painful place. I was jealous of this illness that had become the center of her world instead of me and, but at the time did not even realize it. I did not handle it very well at first. I turned my jealousy into resentment toward her. My wife of six months was damaged and did not even know how to love herself or me. While reading the Bible several months later (I told you I was stubborn), I found a scripture that told me what I needed to do and where I needed to be. Ephesians 5: 23 & 25 "For the husband is the head of the wife, even as Christ is the head of the church: and he is the savior of the body" "Husbands, love your wives, even as Christ also loved the church, and gave himself for it;" God wanted me to sacrifice my wants and needs for my wife. This turned out to be the major part of healing my selfishness! He wanted me to take the lead and be the man she needed me to be for her to lean on. So, for over a year I was her caretaker and God, in his wisdom, had me absorb her anger and fear as well as my anger, and quietly walk away time after time. Did I get frustrated? You had better believe it. Did I get angry? Oh, yes. But it is one of the best things that ever happened to me.

It's easy for other things to take center stage in our homes. Career, children, hobbies and even the church can get out of priority. In Chapter 7, we are going to simulate the perfect family, but right now, we want to identify our adversary. If we put our career or these other things as the first focus of our lives, we have made an idol that will cost us dearly. Remember Mark 12:30? God said He was to be first, our spouse second and others before ourselves. There are a lot of books that will help you with this, but it is just easier to take God's word for it. Remember the "dominion" thing. Part of that power is that we get to determine the priorities in our home.

If we put our children ahead of our spouse, we are harming our marriage and our children. This breeds jealousy in our spouse and teaches our children to misalign their homes when their time comes. If you really love your children, you will do everything in your power to insure they are prepared for life now and eternally, and that means they must see you live it, not just talk about it. I watched my parents wrestle for superiority until I could not stand it anymore and I walked out. Their misalignment carried over into my first marriage and almost into my second. Get some of the books in the "Boundaries" series and learn how to get your priorities straight.

In the movie "Courageous," Nathan talks about the pain of growing up without a father. The sad truth is that there are many homes where "dad" is not present because of his priorities: job, golf, fishing, extra-marital affairs etc. This leaves his wife and children drowning in a pool of jealousy and wounded for life. I wish there were a kinder way for me to say this, but there isn't. Our society, with all its tragedy and pain, is our own doing. It is very easy for that jealousy to bring in all kinds of evil spirits including anger and outright hatred that will become misery in innocent lives.

We are all appalled at the bullying in our schools, but that bullying pales in comparison to the bullying of our own parents when they make other things more important than their own children. It is my belief that if you could get inside the homes of those bullies you would find parents that were out of alignment and the "bully" learned his trade at home. Again, this is not about BLAME. I only want you to understand the results of Satan's spirits in our homes. The bottom line on jealousy is that the husband should lead and love his wife and family the way God instructs him. Wives should honor and nurture their family as God instructs them.

We could go on and on for page after page about each evil spirit, but the truth is they are all the result of selfishness. And simply put, selfishness is the self-inflicted disease where we put ourselves ahead of God and others.

Regardless of the evil spirit you find in your home, the Bible has identified it and the good spirit with which to replace it.

NOTES

NOTES

Defeating the Enemy Within

*I*N this chapter, we are going to learn how to call out the spirits in our home. We do that with accountability. We are accountable for everything we think, do, or say, including the ones we think we got away with. Proverbs 1:31,32 says, "Therefore shall they eat of the fruit of their own way, and be filled with their own devices. For the turning of the simple shall slay them, and the prosperity of fools shall destroy them." What God is saying here is that what we don't dispose of properly is going to destroy us. In Proverbs 15:3 "The eyes of the Lord are in every place, beholding the evil and the good." So now you understand that you can't really hide anything. In one verse, he is saying that our wickedness will destroy us and in the other, he is saying he sees it all, good or bad. The good news is that we cannot break anything that God cannot fix. The only requirement is that you stand up and be accountable for yourself.

After searching for answers for months in the early stages of our healing, I became frustrated because no one could tell us what to do. I went outside in the back yard one day (thank goodness we live out in the country) and I screamed at the top of my lungs at God. I wanted to quit because nothing was working and I was angry. I told him he had the wrong guy and I wanted out. I said, "Get her out of my house, out of my life, I can't do this!" I blurted out all my shortcomings about my selfishness, my sexuality, and all my weaknesses and why I was unqualified. After my temper tantrum subsided, I heard a soft voice in my head say "Finally." All God wanted from me was to stand up and tell the truth about myself for the first time in my life. He wanted me to be accountable for my past and present to Him so he could heal me and lead me to a wonderful new future. Some of you did not get that. Accountability is the ability to tell God and others, as necessary, the truth about ourselves. Accountability is also the ability to recognize our weaknesses and take them to him or others for support before it causes us to fail.

Satan waited until the end of the forty days when Jesus was weak and hungry to tempt him. That is always the case with Satan. Jesus, with a will to serve his father, rebuked

Satan and put him in his place. We are not as strong as Jesus is. Matthew 26:41 "Watch and pray, that ye enter not into temptation: the spirit is indeed willing, but the flesh is weak." He acknowledges that we are weak but he is ready to help any time we ask. Jesus accepted his accountability to his father with no exceptions and wants us to do the same to him. That was the source of his strength, and will be the source of ours.

Let's look at accountability in a way that may surprise and delight you. God is referred to over and over as our "father." For some, that causes us to put him in a box with or compare him with our earthly father. That is normal and we have all done it at one time or another in our lives. That is exactly what the enemy wants us to do.

My grandmother used to tell me "God's going to get you for that." So, as a little boy, I was told God was going to punish me. Like everyone else, I have sat through many sermons about judgment day, hell, and damnation. <u>That is not the God that came to my home and brought his miracle of healing</u>! The word "father" should <u>not</u> bring a feeling of fear.

When I was about eight, I fell in love with baseball. I played every chance I could. I was about ten when several of us, including my brother, went to a vacant lot behind a church in the neighborhood one beautiful summer afternoon to play a game. During the game, I hit a foul ball into a neighbor's yard. It landed in the middle of the windshield of an old car and shattered it. I just stood there and began to tremble because I knew how my parents were going to act when they got the news. Absolute fear wracked my body. Sure enough, that evening the belt was applied to my hind parts.

We did not set out to harm anything, but our actions brought consequences. Did we do something that warranted punishment? If we had been breaking any rules or disobeying our instructions, then yes, we had it coming. Look a little deeper. What past behavior on my father's part led me to believe that I was in trouble? Obviously, things had been handled in the past that put that fear in me. We were boys being boys and were actually behaving ourselves. This was an accident, plain and simple. The sad thing is, I did the same thing to my boys when I became a father.

Now, after that kind of behavior on our part as fathers, we take our children to church and teach them that our "Heavenly Father" is a kind and loving father. Let that sink in for a moment. (Then we don't understand why our young people don't want any part of him.) We have all sat through many sermons that told us about God's wrath, judgement, and damnation. Those are very real, but only the ones that refuse or divorce him should be concerned about them. The fact of the matter is that He is the perfect, loving, kind, giving God that the Bible says he is! I had put

God in a box as someone that "was going to get me" or was going to punish me. I had never learned how to separate our loving God from my earthly father.

Now, let's uncover the most exciting and wonderful part of the recipe. God, our heavenly Father, loves us more than any of us can even comprehend. Picture yourself as the most loving father that ever lived. You look out in the yard to see several evil bullies attacking your child but you cannot go help them until they call your name. Your child tries to stand up to them only to be defeated repeatedly, falling time after time in pain and tears. Play along with me for a moment. Think about your hurt and anger towards those bullies, what they are doing to your loved one, and what you are going to do just as soon as your name is called. When your child finally calls you, how fast would you go to the rescue? When you finally get there, you would, without a doubt, put them in their place. We are that child and our sinful nature is our bullies.

God is our father. The bullies we fight are inside of us, not on the outside. He loves us more than we even know how to love our own, and he is begging and pleading with us to let him help us defeat our bullies. Unfortunately, we, too often, let the bullies beat us down again and again and then wonder out loud why God is letting this happen. He is standing right beside you as we speak waiting for you to call his name. Here is the part we miss; we have to tell him what the bullies have done to us and what we have let the bullies lead us to do. In other words, we have to admit that our sinful spirit has led us to defeat but now, we are ready to defeat them! That is called accountability! Our loving God does not want any bullies in our life and he will help you cast them into an "uninhabitable place." There is **no** evil spirit that he cannot or will not help you control in your life.

Imagine being wrapped in chains and bound in a dark place for years, then one day you look up and dangling right in front of you is the key that unlocks the chains that sets you free and it has been there the whole time. That key is accountability. John 8:32 say, "And ye shall know the truth, and the truth shall set you free." The recipe has several "catches" in it, and our lack of truth (accountability) before God is refusing to call his name to come to our rescue. I could hardly contain myself when I realized the freedom that I had been searching for years was that easy to find. If you have already been asking and praying for healing in your home and you don't feel the evidence of it, chances are that either one of you or both of you haven't let him see all the broken parts (the whole truth from the inside).

That being said, picture a superhero appearing at your side every time you summoned him (he is always just a prayer away). When he arrives, all he has to do is to order the bullies away from you and they must obey. Jesus will do that every day for us, as many times as we need him to, if we let him. He is not a father that is going to strip off his belt and whip us. All he wants from us is a thank you called "trust and obey." He wants us to praise him with true love and affection and not fear of reprisal. Too many people go to church and try sneak into heaven out of the fear of hell instead of understanding how much he loves and adores us. There are too many preachers and Christians telling others about judgment, hell, and damnation before they talk about how much our Lord really loves us.

A little bad news here, the enemy is not going to quit. The bullies will show up every day. The good news is that after a while, the enemy will quit using some of the spirits that cause you to run to Jesus every time he throws them at you. It is hard to sin and pray at the same time.

If you use this recipe to its fullest and you receive the miracle that Laurie and I received, do not keep your witness to yourself. Go tell others how God put a miracle of healing and protection in your home.

NOTES

_____

_____

_____

_____

_____

_____

_____

_____

_____

_____

_____

_____

_____

_____

_____

_____

_____

_____

NOTES

NOTES

The Perfect Home

*I*AM about to share something absolutely impossible to achieve on earth. That is the perfect man, woman, and child. I wish it could be done, but I am realistic.

Let's follow a male baby from birth to manhood. His parents are disciples of Jesus Christ and are versed in the Bible as to how to raise this child.

For the first two to three years of his life, it is the mother that must nurture and care for him. The father is there to help and to lend an air of security and leadership. As the child begins to become aware of the world around him, the parents are there to guide him and protect him from his own curiosity as well as any outside predators. Because he is human, there are some things inherent from birth. The natural tendency to be selfish is quickly whisked away with love and affection. They present a united front against anything that can defile this precious child. There are never any words of anger or hatred around the child. Around the age of two they know that he must begin to learn discipline and gently, but firmly do what is in his best interest and that, occasionally, does (according to Proverbs) require punishment.

Somewhere around age three, it is time for the mother to begin to step back and hand off leadership to the father. This is done in a seamless manner that allows the child to see how his mother honors her husband, and it is done gradually. By this time, the child has begun to develop his character that will stay with him for the rest of his life. It is at this time that the father's character is most important. The father now starts the process of teaching, mainly by example, what is expected of him. They spend time together playing, talking, and enjoying the growth process together. There are times that he falls short (as we all do) and the father helps him to understand his mistakes and grow from them without any condemnation. The father looks for opportunities to give his son his approval so that he will know the joy of seeking approval from his heavenly father.

As he transitions from toddler to boy, he is given more responsibilities, and the father begins to transfer accountability to him. He is taught the truths of the Bible, and how much God loves him. The father starts the process to hand off his son to the Father.

As the boy becomes a man, his father trains him to be a disciple of Jesus, and how to be the priest of his own home when the time comes. He teaches him about sex, money, power, sin, and all the things we have been studying in this book. He teaches him about the purity God expects before and after marriage. He teaches him how to seek the purpose for his life and how to seek the approval of his new father. He helps him develop his gifting and learn how to use it for the glory of the Lord. This process takes place from age twelve or thirteen to approximately age twenty. By age twenty, his father has helped him understand that his new Father will help lead him to the wife that He has chosen for him. He has also accepted the responsibility that he now has to feed himself spiritually as well as any family that he may be blessed with in the future, and he is well prepared.

Now he becomes the husband and father and knows exactly how to do what is required of him. God leads him to a woman, like the one in the next section, and they start the process all over again.

Now let's take a female child from birth to womanhood using similar parents as the first child.

For the first three years, it is the same for her as for her male counterpart. By approximately age five, she has begun to learn what to look for in a man by the way her father treats her and her mother. She sees a kind and loving knight in armor and desperately begins to seek his approval. She hears her mother talk about living with the man of her dreams and knows that someday it will be her turn.

By about age twelve, it is up to her father to begin to validate her as the woman she is becoming. He and her mother help her to learn how precious her purity is and how to protect it. They help her to learn how to properly handle the power God gives her over her mate and home.

As she grows from girl to a woman, her confidence is bestowed upon her by transferring her accountability to her heavenly Father. She embraces the fact that there is another man out there as good as her father and begins her search. Her father has no worry about her choice because of the example he has set for her. When she finds that man that we built in the first scenario, we start all over again.

Now we have the perfect home. The truth, however, is that Satan is not about to let this happen. What we have instead is what we go home to every day. I gave you the examples above to tell you what God intended your home to be: the original "Garden of Eden." Just because it may be impossible does not mean we cannot reach for it and get as close as we can. In order to achieve the perfect home we would have to give up the freedom to make mistakes and we would not need the love and guidance of God. It is because of our failures that He is just waiting to heal and help us. It's time to start choosing whose recipe you are going to use.

What are you waiting for?

NOTES

BEAUTIFUL WORDS

Beautiful words turns strangers into friends

Beautiful words turns hate into compassion.

Beautiful words turns sorrow into joy.

Beautiful words turns anger into peace.

Beautiful words join two into one before God.

Beautiful words stops families from becoming enemies.

Beautiful words sooths the pain of loss.

Beautiful words calms a desperate soul.

Beautiful words gives the lost a path.

Beautiful words warms the coldest heart.

Beautiful words brings freedom to them that utter them.

Beautiful words turn selfishness into sacrifice.

Beautiful words needs no defense.

Beautiful words hurt only Satan.

Beautiful words are the only answer
you will hear to your prayers.

Beautiful words whispered in Jesus' ear removes your sins.

Beautiful words created the universe.

Beautiful words turns our lives into love.

Love turns our lives into beautiful words.

— Pat Gorman

NOTES

NOTES

NOTES